DISCARDED

BAKER & TAYLOR

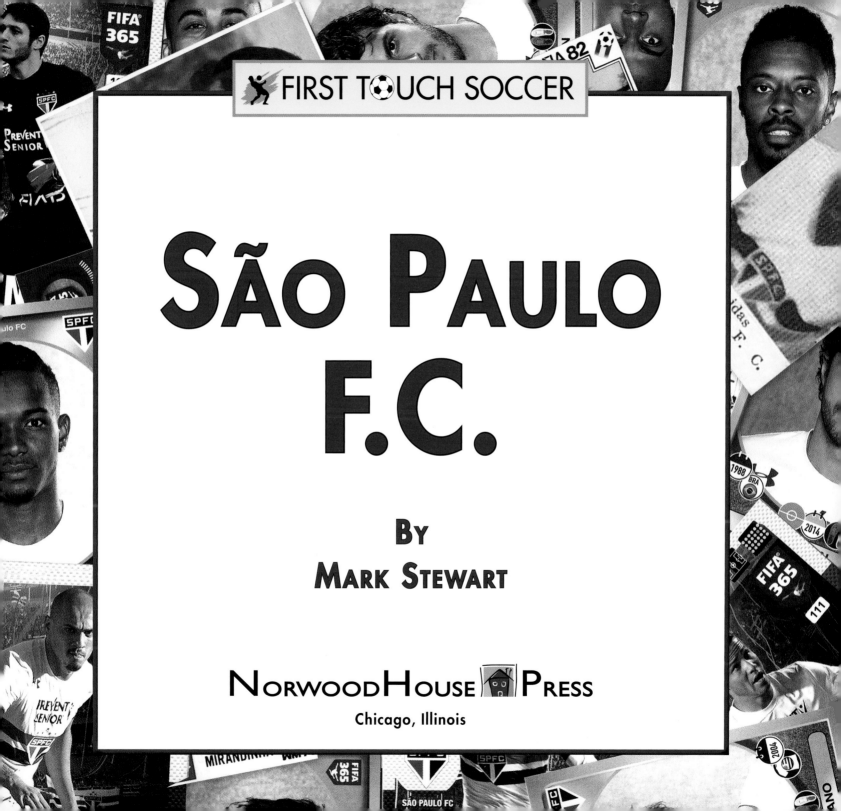

FIRST TOUCH SOCCER

São Paulo
F.C.

By
Mark Stewart

Norwood**H**ouse **P**ress

Chicago, Illinois

NORWOODHOUSE PRESS

P.O. Box 316598 • Chicago, Illinois 60631
For more information about Norwood House Press please visit our website at
www.norwoodhousepress.com or call 866-565-2900.

Photography and Collectibles:
The trading cards and other memorabilia assembled in the background for this book's cover and interior pages
are all part of the author's collection and are reproduced for educational and artistic purposes.

All photos courtesy of Associated Press except the following individual photos and artifacts (page numbers):
Author's Collection (6, 10 top, 23), O. Tinghalls (10 bottom), F.K.S. Publishers Ltd. (11 top),
Figurine Panini (11 middle), Panini SpA (11 bottom), Topps, Inc. (16), The Upper Deck Company LLC (22).

Cover image: Andre Penner/Associated Press

Designer: Ron Jaffe
Series Editor: Mike Kennedy
Content Consultants: Michael Jacobsen and Jonathan Wentworth-Ping
Project Management: Black Book Partners, LLC
Editorial Production: Lisa Walsh

LIBRARY OF CONGRESS CATALOGING-IN-PUBLICATION DATA
Names: Stewart, Mark, 1960 July 7- author.
Title: São Paulo F.C. / By Mark Stewart.
Other titles: São Paulo Futebol Clube
Description: Chicago Illinois : Norwood House Press, 2017. | Series: First
    Touch Soccer | Includes bibliographical references and index. | Audience:
    Age 5-8. | Audience: K to Grade 3.
Identifiers: LCCN 2016058203 (print) | LCCN 2017005794 (ebook) | ISBN
    9781599538686 (library edition : alk. paper) | ISBN 9781684040872 (eBook)
Subjects: LCSH: São Paulo Futebol Clube--History--Juvenile literature.
Classification: LCC GV943.6.S26 S74 2017 (print) | LCC GV943.6.S26 (ebook) |
    DDC 796.334/6409
LC record available at https://lccn.loc.gov/2016058203

302N--072017
Manufactured in the United States of America in North Mankato, Minnesota.

CONTENTS

Words in **bold type** are defined on page 24.

In soccer, star players often go by a one-word nickname. In this book, we use the nickname followed by the player's (*full name*).

São Paulo players lift Rogerio Ceni so he can wave to the fans. The club's beloved goalkeeper played his farewell match in 2015.

Meet São Paulo F.C.

Soccer is king in São Paulo, Brazil's largest city. The São Paulo Futebol Clube is one of Brazil's best. In Brazil, where the language is Portuguese, when people say "futebol" they are talking about the game of soccer, not American football.

São Paulo players are proud to wear the club's red, white, and black uniforms. The best players often leave to play for richer teams. But they never forget their São Paulo roots.

TIME MACHINE

In the 1930s, Brazil was crazy for sports. During this time, São Paulo's soccer club became one of the nation's best. São Paulo has won the **Brazilian League** many times, including three years in a row from 2006 to 2008. The club's great players include Leonidas da Silva, **Serginho (*Sergio Bernardino*)**, Rogerio Ceni, and Luis Fabiano.

SERGINHO

SÃO PAULO F.C.

Luis Fabiano prepares to make his move during a 2004 match. He was known for his great ball control.

7

The great midfielder Kaka (*Ricardo Izecson Santos Leite*) waves to the fans in Morumbi Stadium after a 2014 match.

BEST SEAT IN THE HOUSE

São Paulo plays its home games in a stadium named after Cicero Pompeu de Toledo. He was the club's boss in the 1940s. Most fans call it Morumbi Stadium because it is in the city's Morumbi area. The club has called this field home since 1947. It holds more than 67,000 fans.

COLLECTOR'S CORNER

These collectibles show some of the best São Paulo players ever.

LUISINHO

Forward

1930–1935 & 1941–1947

Luisinho (*Luis Mesquita de Oliveira*) was one of Brazil's top goal-scorers in the 1930s and 1940s. He scored 173 goals for São Paulo.

JOSE POY

Goalkeeper

1948–1962

Poy was a daring goalkeeper for São Paulo. He later became the club's **manager**.

Poy
Sao Paulo F. C.
Brasilien

PEDRO ROCHA

Midfielder/Forward

1970–1977

Rocha was a star in Uruguay before joining São Paulo. He helped the club win its first Brazilian title in 1977.

CARECA

CARECA

Striker

1983–1987

Careca (*Antonio de Oliveira Filho*) scored 54 goals in 67 games for São Paulo. He went on to have a great career in Italy.

DIEGO LUGANO

Defender

2003–2006 & 2016

Lugano's tough defense helped the team win the **Club World Championship** in 2005. Fans were thrilled when he returned to São Paulo in 2016.

WORTHY OPPONENTS

Four great soccer teams play in the state of São Paulo. All are fierce rivals. The São Paulo club has played Palmeiras, Corinthians, and Santos more than 250 times each. Fans call the rivalry between Santos and São Paulo "San-São." As the two best teams in Brazil, they often meet in major tournaments.

A Santos player tries to keep Kaka away from the ball. Millions of fans watch the San-São matches.

13

CLUB WAYS

The fans and players in São Paulo have a special connection. As young people, most everyone plays soccer, dances the samba and learns capoeira. Capoeira is a kind of Brazilian martial art. You can see all of these moves on the soccer field when São Paulo plays. It helps the fans truly get into the game.

São Paulo fans are loud and proud. They believe the players are part of one big family.

These São Paulo players went on to star for top clubs all over the world:

1. **Denilson (*Denilson Pereira Neves*)**
   Arsenal F.C. • London, England

2. **Kaka** • A.C. Milan • Milan, Italy

3. **Ricardo Rocha** • Real Madrid C.F. • Madrid, Spain

4. **Lucas Moura**
   Paris Saint-Germain • Paris, France

5. **Diego Lugano** • Fenerbahce S.K. • Istanbul, Turkey

6. **Souza (*Jose Ivanaldo de Souza*)**
   Krylia Sovetov • Samara, Russia

7. **Nelsinho Baptista** • Kashiwa Reysol • Kashiwa, Japan

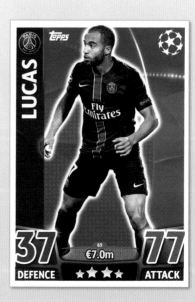

MAP OF EUROPE

São Paulo's home stadium is in São Paulo, Brazil.

1

4

2

3

6

5

7

WORLD MAP

It's hard to miss the big red-white-and-black crest on the front of Jonathan Calleri's uniform.

KIT AND CREST

São Paulo players wear white shirts with a black and red stripe across the chest for home games. These are also the three colors of São Paulo's state flag. The team's away kit is a red shirt with black and white stripes. The team's crest is a shield with the letters SPFC. They stand for São Paulo Futebol Clube.

WE WON!

Most of the club's great victories have come on their home soil. However, one of the best happened half a world away. São Paulo beat mighty Liverpool 1–0 to win the Club World Championship in 2005. The tournament took place in Yokohama, Japan. Mineiro (*Carlos Luciano da Silva*), the team's quiet midfielder, scored the winning goal.

Mineiro celebrates his goal in the 2005 Club World Championship. It was the only goal in an exciting victory over Liverpool.

For the Record

These São Paulo stars have been finalists for South American Footballer of the Year:

1986   Careca • Runner-up

1992   **Rai (*Rai Souza Vieira de Oliveira*)**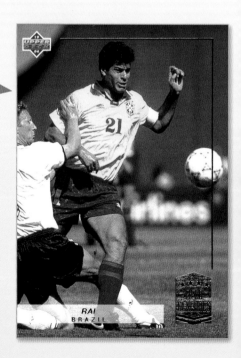
Winner

1993   Cafu (*Marcos Evangelista de Morais*)
Third Place

2005   Diego Lugano • Runner-up

2005   Cicinho (*Cicreo Joao de Cezare*)
Third Place

2012   Lucas Moura • Third Place

São Paulo has won more than 30 championships!

São Paulo League

21 championships (from 1934 to 2006)

Club World Championship

2005

Brazilian League

1977	2006
1986	2007
1991	2008

Copa Libertadores*

1992
1993
2005

Intercontinental Cup

1992
1993

Copa Sudamericana*

2012

Arthur Friedenreich led the club to its first league title in 1931.

Winners of these tournaments were crowned champions of South America.

Brazilian League
The 20-team national league of Brazil. Fans call it the Campeonato Brasileiro or Brasileirão, for short.

Club World Championship
A tournament played each year among the top soccer teams in the world. It is now called the Club World Cup.

Manager
The person who runs a soccer team during games, like a basketball coach or baseball manager in the U.S.

Photos are on **BOLD** numbered pages.

About the Author
Mark Stewart has been writing about world soccer since the 1990s, including *Soccer: A History of the World's Most Popular Game*. In 2005, he co-authored Major League Soccer's 10-year anniversary book.

About São Paolo F.C.
Learn more at these websites:
www.medium.com/são-paulo-fc-english
www.fifa.com
www.teamspiritextras.com